MAMBAS

by Jaclyn Jaycox

PEBBLE
a capstone imprint

Pebble Explore is published by Pebble, an imprint of Capstone.
1710 Roe Crest Drive
North Mankato, Minnesota 56003
www.capstonepub.com

**Library of Congress Cataloging-in-Publication data is available on
the Library of Congress website.**
ISBN 978-1-9771-3198-0 (library binding)
ISBN 978-1-9771-3300-7 (paperback)
ISBN 978-1-9771-5460-6 (eBook PDF)

Summary: Text describes mambas, including where they live, their bodies,
what they do, and dangers to mambas.

Image Credits
Alamy: Avalon/Photoshot License, 25; Capstone Press, 6; iStockphoto:
1001slide, 8, tirc83, 7; Nature Picture Library: Michael D. Kern, 22; Science
Source: Karl H. Switak, 17; Shutterstock : Chedko, 27, Forest man72, 5,
Heiko Kiera, 9, Karl van der Westhuizen, 18, NickEvansKZN, Cover, 1, 11,
OrodO, 12, reptiles4all, 15, Richard Whitcombe, 28, Robert Styppa, 14;
SuperStock: Adrian Warren/Pantheon, 21

Editorial Credits
Editor: Hank Musolf; Designer: Dina Her; Media Researcher:
Morgan Walters; Production Specialist: Tori Abraham

All internet sites appearing in back matter were available and accurate
when this book was sent to press.

Table of Contents

Words in **bold** are in the glossary.

Amazing Mambas

What is one of the fastest and deadliest snakes on Earth? A mamba!

Mambas are a type of **reptile**. They are cold-blooded. They can't control their body heat. If it's hot outside, they are hot. If it is cold, they are cold.

There are four kinds of these snakes. They are the eastern green, western green, Jameson's, and black mambas.

eastern green mamba

Where in the World

Mambas are found in Africa. They live south of the Sahara Desert. They are found in rain forests and woodlands. They also live on rocky hills and in flat, grassy areas.

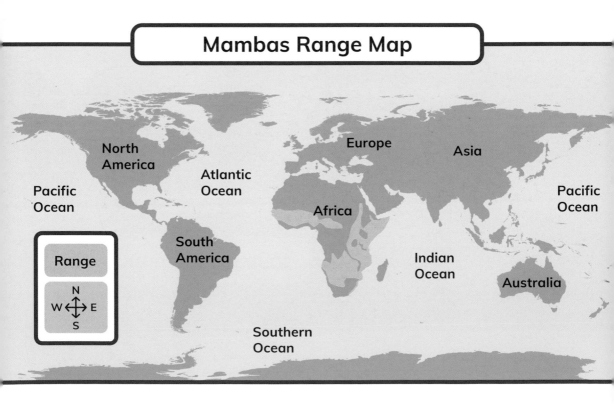

Mambas Range Map

black mamba

These snakes live in warm areas. They need the heat to stay warm. They lay in the sun during the day. If it gets too hot, they cool off in the shade.

Black mambas live on the ground. They make homes in insect mounds and empty **burrows**. They also curl up in hollow trees.

Other types of mambas stay high above the ground. They live in trees or shrubs. They usually only go to the ground to hunt or find water.

Mamba Bodies

Mambas are covered in **scales**. Each type of snake looks a little different.

Black mambas are dark brown, tan, or gray. The skin is lighter under their bellies. The skin inside their mouths is black. That is where they get their name.

Black mambas are the longest **poisonous** snakes in Africa. Most will grow to about 8 feet (2.4 meters) long. Some have grown as long as 14 feet (4.3 m).

black mamba

eastern green mamba

Other mambas are green. Eastern green and western green mambas are bright green. Jameson's mambas are dull green. They blend in with the trees. Their long, thin bodies move easily along branches.

Green mambas are smaller than black ones. Most grow to be between 5 and 6.5 feet (1.5 and 2 m) long. Females are a little longer than males.

Black mambas are the fastest snakes in the world. They can move up to 12.5 miles (20 kilometers) per hour! They use their speed for escaping, not chasing. If they sense danger, they slither away. They only bite if they feel cornered.

Mambas have long, hollow **fangs** that pop out when they bite. **Venom** flows through them. Black mambas are the deadliest. A human can die within 20 minutes of being bitten by one.

On the Menu

Mambas are hunters. They eat mice, bats, and birds. They eat frogs, lizards, and eggs too.

These snakes hunt during the day. They can see very well. Most of them go out looking for food. They slowly sneak up on **prey**. Then they snatch them!

Eastern green mambas hunt differently. They usually wait for prey to come nearby. Then they attack!

A mamba's fangs lay flat in its mouth. When it bites, they pop up. Venom goes into the prey. The snake waits for the animal to die before eating it.

Mambas eat animals whole. Their jaws can open very wide. They swallow animals up to four times bigger than their heads. Their **saliva** helps to break down the food.

Life of a Mamba

Mambas are shy snakes. They live alone. They only come together to **mate**. They usually mate in the spring and summer. Females leave a scent to attract males. Males will travel far to find them.

Sometimes males fight for a mate. They wrap their bodies around each other. They push each other down. One will give up. The winner mates with the female.

two males fighting

newly hatched eastern green mamba

Green mambas lay their eggs in hollow trees. Black mambas lay eggs in burrows or insect mounds. Most times mambas lay around 10 eggs. Some can lay up to 25.

Females hide their eggs from **predators**. They lay them where they will stay warm and dry. Then they leave their eggs. They do not protect them.

The eggs hatch in two to three months. The babies are very small. Newborn green mambas are only about 12 to 15 inches (30 to 38 centimeters) long. Black mambas are a little bigger.

The babies are born with venom. After hatching, they leave the nest. They can hunt on their own. They can catch animals the size of a small rat.

The babies grow very fast. They double in size in the first year. These snakes live 11 to 20 years in the wild.

baby mambas hatching

Dangers to Mambas

A few animals hunt mambas. Small meat-eating animals called mongooses hunt young mambas. Large eagles hunt adults. Doglike animals such as foxes and jackals will eat them too.

Humans are one of the biggest threats to mambas. They are cutting down forests. The snakes are losing their homes.

African black-backed jackal

Humans clear forest land for farming. This means more humans come in contact with these snakes. People kill them because they are scared.

Some people are trying to help save mambas' homes. They are working to protect the land for these snakes.

Fast Facts

Name: mamba

Habitat: tropical rain forests, woodlands, rocky hills, grassy areas

Where in the World: Africa

Food: mice, bats, birds, frogs, lizards, eggs

Predators: mongooses, large eagles, foxes, jackals, humans

Life Span: 11 to 20 years

Glossary

burrow (BUHR-oh)—a hole in the ground made or used by an animal

fang (FANG)—a long pointed tooth; venom flows through fangs

mate (MATE)—to join together to produce young

poisonous (POI-zuhn-uhss)—able to harm or kill

predator (PRED-uh-tur)—an animal that hunts other animals for food

prey (PRAY)—an animal hunted by another animal for food

reptile (REP-tile)—a cold-blooded animal that breathes air and has a backbone; most reptiles have scales

saliva (suh-LYE-vuh)—the clear liquid in the mouth

scale (SKALE)—one of the small pieces of hard skin covering the body of a fish, snake, or other reptile

venom (VEN-uhm)—a poisonous liquid produced by some animals

Read More

Gagne, Tammy. *Snakes: Built for the Hunt.* North Mankato, MN: Capstone Press, 2016.

Lewis, Clare. *Why Do Snakes and Other Animals Have Scales?* Chicago: Heinemann Raintree, 2016.

Murray, Julie. *Black Mambas.* Minneapolis: Abdo Zoom, 2018.

Internet Sites

Kiddle: Mamba Facts for Kids
kids.kiddle.co/Mamba

National Geographic Kids: Super Snakes
kids.nationalgeographic.com/explore/nature/super-snakes/

SoftSchools.com: Black Mamba Facts
softschools.com/facts/animals/black_mamba_facts/324/

Index